TEACHING EXCELLENCE

DR DHEERAJ MEHROTRA JANAKA KAMALGODA

Contents

Preface

Teaching Excellence is a step toward Teaching Standards and practices in schools globally. The book features ideas and strategies toward excellence in teaching and learning post the PANDEMIC globally. Learning as a quality notion is reflected with new ideas on the move and defines the tech culture as a priority among the learners and teachers in totality.

I am looking forward to queries online.

Best

Authors!

CHAPTER ONE

Post Pandemic: Challenges & Preparedness

Taking control of the scenario, we need to build up our emotions and thoughts to stay positive. This has to be the key to dealing with the anxiety amid the COVID-19 pandemic. The priority goes with the inception of protection of our personal space and staying away from the negative news as the new normal.

Friends, we all are affected by the pandemic, and it has had a devastating impact on our community. The business is being shut down, and the schools, colleges and offices are being closed owning to the lockdown. The induced lockdown impacted the economy as severacompanieses were hit. The educators have come out to rescue via the Social and Emotional Learning and Teaching to the students and the community as parents. The teachers are constantly looking for better ways to motivate, engage and teach students, whether the students are in class or at home. If we do not act well and respond to the alarming loss of our children, the loss of our children will prove to be a loss for three years in a row. We, at this moment, introduce the challenges, best practices, available tools and resources to overcome the impact of covid-19 on the education sector. The enriching contributions by some of the education leaders relate to the learning and a take away from the pandemic a new model to the new normal in particular.

As Guest Writers, we share a few findings by educators below on a global scenario,

STAYING MOTIVATED DURING CHALLENGING TIMES

Though the onslaught of Covid has been seriously impacting many lives the world over, the fear, the panic, the mistrust, and the suspicion created alongside their toll on the human psyche. Many people lost their inner strength, enthusiasm, and sense of enterprise and sensed gloom. It reminds me of the famous saying of Leon Trotsky, "You may not be interested in the war, but the war is interested in you" As true warriors, we need to rise and stay motivated. Nobody can motivate us unless we choose to do it for ourselves. Says Robin Sharma, noted author and speaker, "No one can defeat you unless you are defeating yourself". How do we motivate ourselves? It is essential to understand that each has excellent latent power within us, and we have to unlock the potential within.

You have a passion for writing poetry or a story. You don't have to get it celebrated in a magazine, but the fact that you have unleashed your power of fantasy and imagination will give you a sense of achievement and happiness.

You are interested in music. Enjoy your tunes and rhythm, not because you will be branded a superhero on a screen, but you declare yourself as a superhero of your own life, every song of yours will be your soul's message, and you will find how rich you are! You have a reading habit. You won't find a better time to hug your books and plunge into their depth to discover the treasure of centuries of wisdom. You will not only acquire but conquer friends seen and unseen for ages, who will not only talk to you

but counsel you to uplift your morale. You are a techno-maniac. Hey! It is time to unravel the world of knowledge and skills through the portals of your computers. You will wander through many parts of the globe just from your place and at no cost!
Upgrade your understanding of this universe and the people. In all these exercises and several others, you attempt to bridge your "Being with Becoming". It will be a fabulous experience. We are blessed with a time for reflection, re-engineering and redefining our life. Get Set and Go! Never succumb to fear and gloom! Says R.W. Emerson, "The creation of a thousand forests is in one acorn" That is the power of a human being. He adds, "What lies behind you and what lies in front of you pales compared to what lies inside you". It is time to unravel the treasure within!

G. Balasubramanian

Keeping Yourself Motivated during the current scenario!

Motivation is an innate drive which enables you to break the cliché and move ahead with a positive affirmation. The unprecedented times brought the world to a steering halt. Everything seemed topsy turvy, and a whirlpool of negative emotions pushed individuals into an echo chamber of uncertainty, anxiety and fear. I believe in the power of the mind; in fact, it all begins from the mind, as you think; so, shall be. While the outer world slowed down, the inner world started an empathetic journey with a grateful heart. Collaboration, handholding and learning from one another became the new norm, and people from across the globe began collaborating and sharing their expertise. While the world was fighting against covid, the webinars kept people busy, taking them to new learning landscapes. While there was enough stimulation for the mind to learn, keeping and staying fit became the need of the hour; a healthy mind, healthy body, positive thoughts and giving back to society, helping the ones who are less privileged became the norm to fight back and to overcome the prevailing situation. A growth mindset helped me set my sails during the worst times, and my journey from unlearning, relearning and learning kept pushing me to the new terrains of life. I firmly believe that every situation has a solution; there is a light at the end of the tunnel. All we need to do is hold on to hope and be true to ourselves and our work. Be like a river and keep on making your way, keep on flowing, keep on moving ahead, breaking all barriers...and while driving, forward is the only direction. Further, the person in the mirror motivated me, inspired me, questioned me and led me to do more, to be more & to achieve more because woods are lovely dark and deep, but I have promises to keep and miles to go before I sleep...& miles to go. As an educator, the disaster-driven digitalisation changed the learning landscapes in the parent's shoes while they stepped into educators. We are riding on the tide of a culture of constant change.

Last but not least, feed your mind with positivity and wisdom. Discipline is a must in life, and prioritising yourself needs to be at the top of every day's to-do list. I follow a simple routine I practice gratitude and empathy, which keeps me mentally and emotionally calm. One hour of physical exercise 5 days a week is a ritual. Also, when you make the mirror your most prominent critic, you are very well known for what you want to see. So, be the best version of yourself, mentally and physically, emotionally, and lookup for opportunities amidst the adversities; all we need to do is change our lenses to see that life is beautiful. We need to live it to the fullest every day.

Dr Seema Negi

I am beating Covid my way.

When I reflect upon the year, I see it as a year of great learning. I have always believed that learning never ends because life never stops teaching us. This Covid time has reinforced that and taught me resilience, collaboration, communication and critical thinking. It has helped me push my limits and discover more. Most importantly, it gave me an insight into various nuances of life and the time to reflect and look inwards. Education has evolved and given wings of opportunities to today's learners. The seamless transition of my school to the online mode is proof of that. The rigours were felt and dealt with, and the transformation into online classes, activities, interactions, learning tools, resources, massive open online free courses and apps came to the rescue of students. Today there is no shortage of possibilities, even when the student body remains confined to their homes. Indeed, ourareirit has been tested,t we emerged victoriously; the institution and I have worked in tandem. Our desire to give the students a wholesome education has blessed us with positivity and hope. We grow each day, replicating all school activities online with the same spirit and value as the offline ones. Online classes have been enriched with ICT tools and suggested hands-on activities. School competitions and co-curricular activities like debates, talent fests, MUNs, Sports Day, Class wise presentations and orientations were successfully conducted. Other important developmental monitoring segments such as Career counselling sessions, Parent-Teacher meetings, and Interaction of students with professional experts were also organised. And are still marching on, undeterred.

Keeping in mind that the continuous lockdowns will deter students from availing of texts, practice workbooks, and papers, we have also worked on our own MOODLE, a robust learning platform or course management system (CMS). It is a software package designed to help educators create adequate online resources for students. My love and passion for remaining in touch with my students inspired me to create an accessible learninbrainpoweri,nPower, which has research-proven strategies that can effectively improve memory, enhance recall, and increase retention of information. I also launched a course about 'training the brain' on Udemy, a MOOC.

Parent-community also needed special attention; hence I started a series of talks on YouTube called 'Parent to Parent-Man Ki Baat' to motivate the parents to develop the resilience to cope with whatever life throws at them and become socially and emotionally intense.

These unprecedented times have taught me like never before, and owing to my determination; I could record, edit, compile and upload all my digital content singlehandedly. The world is battling with new challenges, unlearning and relearning. To keep at it is the key to growth. My firm belief in the power of learning, especially in a storm like Covid, is reiterated in the words of Louisa May Alcott, " I am not afraid of storms for I am learning how to sail my ship."

Dr Anshu Arora

Five most beneficial ways to keep yourself motivated during these difficult times

The COVID-19 pandemic has shaken our lives and the world in many ways. After months of being stuck at home has given birth to several problems. Limited exposure to friends and family members and, most importantly, juggling between home and office responsibilities have resulted in anger, low morale, frustration, and much more. Some studies have shown that a positive outlook and mindset can help balance both mind and body. Being positive is to face challenges with great willpower and helping each other during these unprecedented times. Most of you may find it arduous to keep yourself motivated. But worry not, we are here with the most beneficial ways to keep you positive:

Make a routine- Kick start your day by waking up early and workout to stay positive and energised. Make a to-do list with all the tasks related to work and personal chores you want to accomplish during the day. The to-do list will help you keep track of what needs to be done and help you be prepared for the next day. Paint, sing or read a book- We all have certain hobbies, and this is the best time to begin spending more time doing our favourite things. This will give you much happiness and be quite healing as well. So, why wait? Take out those paintbrushes or a book to get engrossed in your favourite stuff.

Stay calm and relaxed- There is so much going on outside that you need to get offline from all this and breathe. It is not always essential to listen to and watch everything on social media and television. Filter out things and spend your valuable time listening to good songs, watching movies, cooking, etc. Take time to appreciate nature, walk in your garden, and spend some quality time with your family.

Schedule virtual get-togethers- Yes, your friends and family members are the most important people in your life. Meeting them is not possible these days, but you can talk to them through video calls and feel great. Plan out the time and make the best use of the same to play games and chit-chat. These little joys will make you happy and motivated.

Prioritise your mental health- Staying positive during these times can be difficult. But, if we continue doing this, it can be harmful to our mental health. Exercise, talk to your friends and family, read books and have a good diet. Taking care of yourself is the foremost thing. Stay positive to beat the odds as you can do it. It is not too late; prep up yourself and creates a beautiful and cheerful world for yourself. There is no benefit in sitting and worrying about things, as it will only toll your mental health. Do not forget that you have come this far. You are stronger than you think!

Remember, this too shall pass!

Dr Sangeeta

KEEPING YOURSELF MOTIVATED DURING THIS PANDEMIC

A pessimist sees a problem in every opportunity, and an optimist sees an opportunity in every situation.

No one is exempted from the trials and tribulations of life, yet it is up to us how we look at things and situations. Life has never been fair. Poetic justice never seems to reign in real life. It is a far fetched notion that appears to prevail only in fiction. So how can we change our situations whilst we have no control over them. Can't we remould the way we think and perceive things. There is a way out of falling into the ditch of depression from where a comeback may be challenging. We can always try to find something positive even in the worst of situations. Is it that difficult?

The Covid Pandemic is one of its kind. It has disrupted and corroded our smooth going lives. With the clampdown on movements, be it due to a series of lockdowns or sensible self-imposed or forced quarantine, many of us are stuck within the four walls of our home, unable to visit our family and friends. The "work from home" formula seems you have traded our "travelling time" with our ' time'. Many of us have lost our jobs and regular source of income. Schools have been temporarily shut down, leaving parents even more perplexed with household chores and co-educating their kids with teachers. All this has led to a conglomeration of never experienced emotions. Even those who claim to be level headed and emotionally intense have succumbed to the unexpected and unwelcomed whirlpool of poignant situations. Therefore, it is no surprise that thousands and millions of us are wrestling with negative thoughts, grappling with loneliness and dealing with a constant sense of despair and frustration. If you think you are the only one who cannot handle the ongoing situation and live in an environment where there seems to be no ray of hope, you are mistaken.

But wait. There is an option. You always had one. Either you can collapse under the pressure of this pandemic and give up whatever hope you have, or gather that fistful of hope, fight like a warrior and rise like the phoenix.

Let us promise to be a fighter and remember how optimism can tilt the odds in your favour. Let me share a few strategies which will surely help you keep motivated and away from negativity and hopelessness.

Accept the situation and strategies. Acknowledging one's position is the foremost step to getting out of a hostile environment. Gather all your mental and emotional strength and chart out how to come out of it. Don't hesitate to take help from your near and dear ones.

Invest in self-care: The age-old saying a healthy mind lives in a healthy body still stands relevant. Get up, take a walk on your terrace or balcony or within your room, stretch your body, engage yourself in yoga and do light exercises. Inhale positivity and hope with enough oxygen in your lungs and exhale all negative thoughts and keep a smile on your face.

Engage yourself in your favourite activity and Stay Productive. When we engage ourselves in our famous work, we feel relaxed, our mind becomes stable, and a sense of achievement sets in. You can read a book, take care of plants, play with your children, solve Sudoku, decorate your room, groom yourself.... the list is endless.

Talk, express and share your thoughts: Don't stay silent and live in your imaginary world. Rather speak out. It will help to vent out your emotions.

Filter your source of information: News channels are flooded with fake and distressful information. Do watch the news channel but take in only the relevant information and don't allow any negative information to disturb your state of mind.

Try to learn a skill: Learn a new skill from your parent, your sibling or the internet. Learning a new skill will always help bring a sense of achievement and groom you into a better person.

Design a Schedule: A Schedule would help you organise your task and keep you active throughout the day. It would give you enough time to reflect upon your situation.

Make Gratitude your Attitude: Feel blessed to have a life which many others might have been deprived of. Remember, one should never take everything for granted. Cherish and celebrate the small joys of life. This unprecedented pandemic has compelled every one of us to alter our behaviour, whether we like it. The ongoing situation feels endless but believes me, everything has an end, and this will end one day. Above all, remember, Worrying doesn't empty tomorrow of its sorrows, but it opens today of its strengths. So, Keep smiling and stay motivated.

Alka Kapur

Keep yourself motivated even during the current scenario.

You may feel that your life has suddenly flipped upside down, and your motivation is at an all-time low because we are all using social distancing strategies, and most of us are home-based. You're not alone, after all! This, like every other difficult period in history, will pass, and we will emerge stronger. Meanwhile, it's vital to remember that there are methods to keep your mind balanced and motivated even if you're stuck at home.

1. Set simple daily objectives.

It's critical to remember that these aren't regular times, and your performance will not be at its best right now. And that's fine. Setting daily objectives can help you make the most of your day, but be practical with your expectations. Make sure they're not too high, or you'll be disappointed.

2. Make a schedule that includes both work and leisure.

Working from home might make it difficult to resist the desire to operate continuously or to become easily distracted by television or other household items... leading to the sensation that you are not achieving the tasks you set for yourself. You may achieve a healthy work-life balance at home by scheduling when you will work and when you will rest.

3. Make virtual get-togethers with pals a priority.

The worst element of this epidemic might be social separation, especially for folks who appreciate the social side of coming together. But you don't have to stop doing so, and you don't have to give up your social life.

4. Make your mental health a top priority.

You must manage your stress and concerns at this time. If you're having trouble staying motivated, take a look at your hurdles. Make sure you get some exercise every day, even if it's simply a walk around your block or neighbourhood, to keep your mental health in check.

5. Accept that you won't be very productive right now.

Some days, you may discover that you are driven and do more things than you intended, while other days, you are entirely unfocused. It's ok; nothing is expected now, and we all need to pay attention to ourselves. Go over your to-do list and prioritise what needs to be done today against what can wait until tomorrow.

A couple of additional suggestions

Let go of whatever shame you may have felt for not being successful. Take each day as an opportunity to start over. Look for bright moments wherever you can, such as strangers helping strangers, teachers checking in on students, and communities banding together. Consider restricting how much you watch the news or read about the covid-19. If you need help, reach out to those who you trust.

Dr Malka Grewal

***Self Motivation** is the key to unlocking the potential within you. Make things happen !!! Do not give up !!!! Do what you love. Take some time out and talk to yourself. Self-talk helps a lot. Be careful with your word when you speak to yourself. Use positive and inspiring words. Keep appreciating yourself for your excellent work.*

Manage your expectations. Keep small achievable goals. Surround yourself with positive people in their thoughts and words and motivate you. They will help you Reframe, Redirect and Refocus your goals when it gets tricky.

No matter how small your achievement is, celebrate your success. Paint a beautiful vision of your future. Be so self-motivated that you are an inspiration to others.

The best part of this pandemic scenario is how digitalisation has shrunk the world. Thanks to Zoom, MEET, and Teams, connecting with global counterparts has become very easy. Plan online get-togethers and celebrations.

Information is good but limits you to reading pandemic-related news for only a short time but not in the morning. Stay informed from reputable sources, but avoid getting wrapped up in constant news coverage that will only heighten anxiety. Allow yourself time to enjoy TV and social media, but try to reduce how much time you spend listening to pandemic news.

Taking care of yourself can help you better manage your mental health during this time. Maintain a regular sleep schedule, and aim to get at least eight hours of sleep a night. Have a healthy balanced diet and exercise regularly.

Some days you may not have much ability to focus, which is expected! Nobody's life is every day right now. You may find that you have good days where you're highly motivated to get through work and bad days where your motivation is nowhere to be found. It's okay to expect less from yourself right now.

Lockdown!!!! Yes, everyone is locked up !!! But this is the best time to unlock your potential!!! You might be working from home and still trying to maintain a similar routine. Get dressed the way you wud if you had to travel to work.

Don't lose focus on your goals. Force yourself to keep going forward. This, too, shall pass !!!

Dr Ushavati Shetty

KEEPING YOURSELF MOTIVATED EVEN DURING THE CURRENT SCENARIO

2020....The world almost came to a standstill due to the pandemic. The disruption we are facing is unlike anything we have met before. It is legitimate for us to feel frustration, anger, and more due to the multitude of ways our lives have changed. How do we stay motivated right now, more than one year into a pandemic with no end in sight?

CHANGE AND MODIFY YOUR EXPECTATIONS Now is not the time, I would say, to pretend these are typical times. Acknowledging and accepting that it is OK not to feel inspired as we did in 2019 is the first step to helping us adjust to this new normal. Everyone is struggling right now, and the world is going through collective grief. Telling yourself, 'I am not alone in this, and it is perfectly okay not to be highly productive now ' is the first step to having collective motivation to sail through unprecedented times.

STAY CONNECTED Loneliness, isolation and challenges to mental health have been significant by-products of the pandemic, impacting our resilience in these difficult times. Having a support network of friends, family and peers can help people get through these periods of trauma and improve their ability to respond to stress; Remaining connected even at a distance during even the strictest of lockdowns is helpful. Have you ever surprised yourself when walking around, adopting all sanitary norms, by " Oh! I am alive! There are people around me!"? Everything is not doom and gloom. This is motivation to carry on.

TRANSFORM CHALLENGES INTO OPPORTUNITIES A matchless gift given to us by the pandemic is undoubtedly time which can be used to transform challenges into opportunities to innovate, succeed and grow both individually and professionally. The education sector is one of the most impacted ones in current times. Many education stakeholders have remained motivated even globally by connecting through digital platforms during webinars and sharing resources. Building up soft skills during this period through virtual internships and other activities has been a great source of motivation for students. On a personal note, my most remarkable experience has been having my students from Mauritius participate enthusiastically in a virtual MUN Conference hosted by Sri Ram College of Commerce, Delhi University! Create opportunities for yourself with what is globally available.

INVEST IN SELF-CARE Navigating this new normal is not easy, creating a need to motivate ourselves to take care of our health- all aspects of it by investing in simple things that make a huge difference in our mental state.

Prioritising good-quality sleep to keep our immune system running properly

Exercising and adopting healthy eating habits

Doing a creative hobby

Reading (something inspiring helps)

Listening to music

Trying something altogether new to you and above all

Maintaining happiness for yourself and your environment.

We live in an unusually challenging time, but we either succumb to the pressure and give up or stay motivated to get through and come out even better than before.

WHEN ALL IS WELL, WE ARE GOING TO LOOK BACK ON THIS PERIOD OF OUR LIVES AND BE GLAD WE NEVER GAVE UP.

Prabha Doonanath

'Every cloud has a silver lining'.....and we should follow this during this pandemic situation.

Covid-19, of course, is causing havoc, but we should never lose hope. If we think positive, everything becomes positive, and if we keep on thinking about negative things, it becomes harmful. We should keep ourselves busy with different jobs; it may be a household job, hobbies, our passion for gardening, reading books, etc. We should make a timetable ready for us, our daily routine we used to follow before will now slightly change. Previously we often heard people saying that due to my busy schedule, I hardly have time to even speak to my relatives or even give quality time to my family....but now we can. Covid-19 has taught us certain things; earlier, we became too busy with our work, we started maintaining gratuitous associations, but now we are very cautious about hygiene; we hardly physically go out and meet people. We don't mind being house arrested just to save our family members. We can self motivate ourselves:

1. We can set daily targets: It helps us a lot; you feel good as if you did not waste your day at the end of the day. You could achieve what you wanted. It may be straightforward, like arranging your wardrobe, completing five storybook pages, learning a dish, etc.

2. Being socially active: You may meet your friends and relatives through digital meeting platforms, keep in touch, or pursue official jobs. This way, you don't feel lonely and share your feelings with others.

3. Take care of your mental and physical health: You are responsible for your happiness and sadness. Nobody can make you happy or sad. It is your responsibility to keep yourself fit and fine. You should go for exercise every day, eat healthily, drink plenty of water and limit yourself to reading pandemic related news and avoid getting wrapped up in constant news coverage that will only increase your anxiety.

4. Give time to yourself: Whatever makes you happy, Just do it! It may be cooking, watching movies, stitching, playing video games, gardening, painting, gossiping(virtually), or making you feel happy. Go ahead and keep yourself charged.

5. Extending help to others: At this difficult point, it is essential to extend helping hands to others in various ways. Many social activists or NGOs selflessly work day and night to serve society by offering food, oxygen, medicines, and ambulance service, to name a few. By helping others in their difficult time, one can achieve immense happiness. But yes, while extending helps to others, no one should forget to take the necessary self-protection measures.

Last but not least, though it's my personal feeling if anybody requires any sort of help, we may extend it to them, sometimes even some motivating words make a huge difference.

Dr Nandita Nandi

CHAPTER TWO

TEACHING STRATEGIES

Let us all learn about the Importance of Teaching Excellence:

Identifying the Classroom Distractions is a priority for the New Age Learning. As Educators, we need to explore the contest of learning with an exception.

The concern comes to our minds, why use a teaching strategy?

It is more like an Instructional Method that a teacher adopts to meet a learning objective.

It also aids a teacher in creating the right learning environment.

Well, for sure, the teaching methods foster and improve students learning journey. They are essential for students to make learning more conceptual and contextual.

A teaching strategy for a student's friendly classroom need not necessarily be very fancy; it can be engaging, straightforward, and less time-consuming.

To plan the teaching strategies, teachers need to consider the effectiveness and active participation of the students.

As an educator, it is necessary to prepare and set transparent and fair expectations that have a positive attitude, be mindful, and use a teaching strategy that is inquiry-driven, creative, and innovative.

Assure any of your teaching strategies should not be boring. We need to consider the lack of focus among the kids as a priority.

Some of the Teaching Strategies feature as follows:

1. Lecturing

Lecturing can mean an instructional talk, or it can take the form of a stern, one-sided conversation. It is in part through engaging students in interaction, using questions and

answers, that some of the limitations of lectures can be overcome. The course has to be Lively, Educative, Creative, Thought-provoking, Understanding, Relevant and Enjoyable.

2. Circle Time Activities

A Circle time, also called group time, refers to a group of people sitting together for an activity involving everyone. Circle time is usually light and fun and aims to get children ready for learning. Consider the three basic questions of Why, What, and How.

3. Simulation Method

Activating classrooms via Simulations refers to instructional scenarios where the learner is placed in a "world" defined by the teacher. They represent a reality within which students interact. The teacher controls the parameters of this "Engagement" and uses it to achieve the desired instructional results.

4. Modelling Method

Modelling during teaching is an instructional strategy in which the teacher demonstrates a new concept or approach to learning, and students learn by observing. Whenever a teacher explains a concept forto a student, that teacher is modelling. It activates engagement in an absolute sense.

5. Online Learning Tools

These are the Most Popular Digital Education Tools For Teachers And Learners. The most common ones include Edmodo, an educational tool that connects teachers and students and assimilates into a social network. Google Classrooms and Kahoot are other commonly used platforms.

6. Game Simulation

As one of the innovative ways of teaching, the use of simulation games implies that the teacher values the unique needs of individual students. Learning is an active process rather than a passive one during this process. It encapsulates the importance of students‘ examining their values and the values of others in particular.

7. Collaborative Problem Solving

Very collaborative problem-solving acts as "the capacity of an individual to effectively engage in a process whereby two or more agents attempt to solve a problem by sharing the understanding and effort required to come to a solution and pooling their knowledge and skills in totality. It activates learning by doing hands-

on.

8. Discussion Groups

The Discussion method of teaching is a group activity which involves the teacher and the student in defining the problem and deriving its solution. It is a constructive process that involves listening, thinking, and deriving conversation skills on priority.

9. Peer Instruction

Peer teaching involves one or more students teaching other students in a particular subject area and builds on the belief that "to teach is to learn twice" (Whitman, 1998)." For students, peer learning can lead to improved attitudes and a more personalised, engaging, and collaborative learning experience, leading to higher achievement. The experience can deepen their understanding of the subject and impart confidence to peer teachers.

10. Active Learning

Active learning is an approach to instruction that involves actively engaging students with the course material through discussions, problem-solving, case studies, role plays and other methods. The process is towards giving students a time limit to complete the task. The strategy identifies to Stop the activity and debrief. Call on a few students or groups of students to share their thoughts and tie them into the next steps of your lecture.

11. Project-Based Learning

Project-Based Learning is a teaching method in which students gain knowledge and skills by working for an extended period to investigate and respond to an authentic, engaging, and complex question, problem, or challenge. Project-based teachers ensure that students understand the learning goals and why they matter towards catching them young and innocent.

12. Unit Tests

Unit tests are conducted in the school to evaluate the summative assessment of the teaching-learning process. The main aim of the unit test is to isolate each unit of the system to identify, analyse and fix the defects. The test is different from assessment and evaluation in the following manner towards excellence.

13. Assignments

The Assignment method is the most common teaching method in schools, particularly in the teaching of Science. It is a technique usually used in the teaching and learning process. It is an instructional technique that comprises guided information, self-learning, writing skills and report preparation. It also includes simple homework assignments as one of the standard learning and evaluation methods.

14. Classroom Quizzing and Brain Gym:

Ask questions and make their brain work brighter. Example: Ask them to make the number 9 using their thumb altogether. Ask them to write their first name in ENGLISH using their index finger in the air.

15. Remedial Teaching

Identify weak students and engage them through peer learning. Involve them through partners such as 12.00 O Clock Partner or other time frames. This can even happen before assembly or after school.

16. Presentations

Engage them through the presentation skills via Technology. Some widely used presentation platforms include PREZI, MS Powerpoint and KEYNOTE.

17. Zoom In

Let the students observe gradual portions of an image and ask them to write and engage in writing. Ask them what new things they see. How does it change their thinking? Repeat the reveal and questioning until the whole image is revealed.

18. Chalk Talk

Using the Chalk Talk Strategy to engage them via homework analysis. The chalk talk method is an excellent way to ignite shy students. It engages the learners, promotes independent thinking and allows them to have an equal say. Here the teacher tells the students to analyse their thought analysis. The students rotate as a team via different prompts. The output is shared in public.

19. Work Books & Step Inside Routine

It gives the option to students to answer questions using Step Inside virtually. You let them step inside the character of the individuals. It is like stepping inside the situation in particular. Suitable for English, History, and exploring historical events from a specific perspective. Example Thinking or wondering about a soldier's perspective.

20. Posters and Reading Conference

Showcase the Posters and ask the children to read and interact. This goes via interactions randomly with peers and the teachers. It integrates Visual Literacy like I see I wonder. The use of posters and the opportunity to read the content individually or as per the lucky system works wonders.

21. Self-Learning Tools

This is a live example of using learning tools as a practical approach. Some online tools include Google Digital Garage, LinkedIn Learning, Coursera, Khan Academy, edX and Academic Earth.

22. Competitions

This includes the various formats like Debates/ Interactions/ Recitation/ Writing/ Fashion Shows/ Speech Contest/ Case Study Presentations.

23. Object-Based Learning

Object-based learning is a form of active learning. A student-centred learning approach is an educational method that actively actively actively us classroom learning via engagement as a priority. To make it effective, the students must first practice the imparted skills of identifying and describing the main topic or activity in a class and giving some coherent, sequenced details. The idea is to catch them young and innocent towards learning as the ultimate.

25. Club Activities

This leads to bodily awareness, independent thinking, problem-solving and reasoning, positive self-image, talent management and collaboration & teamwork. The other activities include co-curricular activities such as public speaking, debate and dramatics, creative writing, eco-club, quizzing, astronomy, dance, photography, philately, trekking, film appreciation and even cooking.

26. Adaptive Teaching

Adaptive teaching as an educational method aims to achieve a common instructional goal with learners whose individual differences, such as prior achievement, aptitude, or learning styles, differ. It assists in providing personalised learning, aiming at providing efficient, effective, and customised learning paths to the learners. It also helps the teachers to engage each student. It is a student data-driven approach to adjusting the direction and pace of learning, enabling the delivery of personalised learning at scale in totality.

27. Cross Over Learning

The concept of crossover learning refers to a comprehensive understanding of learning that bridges formal and informal learning settings toward teaching excellence. It is one of the techniques used to provide personalised learning and aims to provide efficient, effective, and customised learning paths to engage each student.

28. Case Study

The case study methodology incorporates learning by engaging the students in discussing specific scenarios that represent real-world examples, such as Distractions Within Classrooms. This method is learner-centred, with intense interaction between participants, such as brainstorming. This further makes them develop skills, build their knowledge and work together as a group to examine the case.

29. Self-Learning

Using Google Earth Educational Tools. This helps visualise the abstract concepts across a global canvas, allowing students to connect what they learn inside to what they experience in their daily lives, community, and the larger world. Google Earth's creation tools allow will enable you to create your projects.

30. Team Projects

This may include creating a poster, making a PowerPoint presentation, designing a model, making a shoebox diorama, Using a 3-panel display board, Making a timeline, creating a board game incorporating key elements, and writing a poem.

31. Research Projects

Research-based teaching means that students conduct research independently and with an open outcome in their courses. This teaching and learning methodology focuses on the joint acquisition of new skills by lecturers and students. This requires the teachers to reflect on their role as teachers and learners.

32. Gesturing

This form of teaching integrates the learner's gestures, allowing indexing of conceptual instability moments. The teachers, during this process, make use of those gestures to gain access to a student's thinking. The learners discover novel ideas from the gestures produced during a lesson during the process.

33. Instructional Videos

This is a prevalent methodology to integrate the showcase of learning using videos. The instructions electronically in videos guide the students to follow a specific path, and learning is depicted during the process.

34. Social Media

The ultimate use of social media in teaching assists the students with the ability to get more helpful information. It makes them connected with learning groups and other educational platforms online. It allows the students to share their queries, concerns, and comments, making education convenient. These tools allow the students and institutions to explore multiple opportunities to improve learning methods.

35. Humour

Humour in the classroom explores the inception of Teaching styles that have changed significantly over the years. It allows the switch from the traditional way education was delivered through recitation and memorisation techniques. In contrast, the modern way of doing things involves interactive methods with humour as a priority now for sure with the march of time and tide as a reality in practice for schools and teachers need to dwell as a hobby for now. The inception is eyed and segmented towards the participative nature of students within classrooms to connect and make learning a priority for both the teacher and the learner in momentum to share the cause of education, making the best for all.

36. Panel Discussion

During this teaching process, the process is initiated through observation and listening. In a Panel Discussion, a designated or an invited group of students act as a panel, and the remaining class members act as the audience. The committee further discusses the selected questions and topics in particular. A panel leader is chosen, and they summarise the panel discussion and opens the conversation to the audience. A question and answer session follow the process for clarity and collaboration.

37. Modelling

Modelling is an instructional strategy in which the teacher demonstrates a new concept or an approach to make learning a priority with the preface of teaching excellence and WOW spectrum towards the taste and requirements of the learners. The students during this phase enjoy the learning through observation. The teaching is done by observing. Whenever a teacher demonstrates a concept for a student, that teacher is modelling as a measure.

38. Discovery Method

The Discovery Learning Method is mandated through the "Guided Discovery" format, which refers to a teaching and learning environment where students actively discover knowledge by exploring options through working and exploring ideas. It is a constructivist theory based on the idea that students construct their understanding and knowledge of the world by experiencing things and reflecting on those experiences. It is assisted through inquiry-based instruction and is considered a constructivist-based education approach.

39. Demonstration Method

As the word says, demonstration, the module covers showcasing with explanation in particular. It is used to communicate an idea with the assistance of visuals like flip charts, posters, PowerPoint, and other online or offline tools. A demonstration is a process of teaching someone how to make or do something step-by-step. It is suitable for science subjects.

40. Role Playing Method

Role-play is a technique that allows students to explore realistic situations by interacting with other people in an organised manner towards developing real-life skills and experiencing an environment of choice and chance. It provides an additional learning delight for the students, and they can very well understand the scenario being discussed during the process.

41. Oral Questions

This methodology allows the teacher to engage the students via assignments orally. It initiates and involves the teacher, where probing is conducted among the students. Here the questions are floated to think about what they know regarding a topic, and in the verbal format, they respond. The Questions typically allow the teacher to keep a point of the discussion focused on the intended objective and the learning objective through the involvement of all the students at length.

42. Questioning Method

This is an add on the method to the Oral Questions and may include the written assignments. The objective is to engage the students via connections and jobs.

43. Discussion Method

Here we follow the collaborative exchange of ideas among the students to ignite students thinking, learning, problem-solving, understanding, and decision-making abilities.

44. Problem Based Learning

This identifies the engagement of the kids through Question or Assignment based learning. The teacher takes the problem/ assignment and works on it with the students and significant contributors. This acts as one of the easy-going tools to examine them during revision modules.

45. Assignments

This includes work assignments, routine jobs, class tests, homework and online reflections.

46. Make free and open source technologies available to teachers and students

The objective is towards specific connections via the directions from the UNESCO, Open educational resources and open access digital tools must be supported. Education cannot thrive with ready-made content built outside of the pedagogical space and outside of human relationships between teachers and students. Nor can education be dependent on digital platforms controlled by private companies.

47. Cross Over Learning

The crossover learning format entirely refers to a comprehensive understanding of learning that bridges a classroom's formal and informal learning settings. Experiences from everyday life can enrich the learning through this medium; informal learning can be deepened by adding questions and knowledge from the school. This format aims to combine the strengths of formal and informal learning environments and seeks to provide students with the best of both. As per boardteachers.com, an effective method for crossover learning involves teachers proposing a question or problem in the classroom to be solved during museum visits or field trips. Children can learn by collecting photos, taking down notes, or asking other people for their thoughts. They then present what they learned back in the classroom to illuminate the given problem further.

48. Dramatic Method

It is more like drama in teaching or dramatics in education. This, at random, allows students to explore the curriculum using several of Gardner's multiple intelligences. Here the kids are fully involved in learning with drama as a practice. They are immersed in the subject through the activities and do role plays of characters on the subject of learning. The process activates at length the development of their skills and, particularly, their bodies, minds, and emotions, yielding creativity and innovation as a common practice.

49. Pen Pals

A coined word of yesteryears has an interpreted meaning today. Teachers and educators worldwide share their experience with global project-based learning through PenPal platforms. One of the schools practising this says: We set the children up with their email addresses and put these under one central email alias. This allowed the teachers to screen each email exchange to ensure it was appropriate and then prepare spelling lists and topic word banks based on the sales. We moved to weekly discussions because the messages were now arriving within seconds of hitting "send," and we moved to weekly deals. This allowed our students to breeze through the usual "getting to know you" questions and move on to topics that allowed for meaningful cultural interactions.

50. Audio Tutorial Lessons

Also known as PODCASTING in a novel sense, the format is widely used in schools. The audio tutorial instruction is the most complete and well-documented auditory presentation method among teachers.

51. Mobile Applications

Mobile apps help in systematic learning in a big way. The best part is that Mobile learning (m- learning) is education via the Internet with the help of personal mobile devices. This is encompassed with BYOD- Bring Your Device format in schools where devices like tablets and smartphones assist learning to a better level. It helps obtain learning materials through mobile apps, social interactions and online educational hubs.

52. Flowcharts

This is a diagrammatic way of teaching where each activity is represented through a symbol. These are joined through the direction arrows and are connected through lines.

53. Brain Storming

This is an act of idea generation. This activity encourages students to focus on a topic and contribute to the free flow of ideas. Ideally, it is initiated by the teacher as a facilitator who may begin a brainstorming session by posing a question or a problem or by introducing a topic. In-process, the students express possible answers, relevant words, and ideas.

54. Simulation Games

The use of simulation games within classrooms implies that the teacher values the unique needs of individual students. It signifies that learning is an active process and hence has to equip with innovation and creativity.

55. Psychomotor Development Methods

Psychomotor learning is demonstrated by physical skills such as movement, coordination, and manipulation of learning traits among students. It delivers organised patterns of muscular activities guided by signals from the environment.

56. Inquiry Method

Inquiry-based learning is an approach that encapsulates the student's role in the learning process. Rather than the teacher telling students what they need to know, students are encouraged to explore the material, ask questions, and share ideas.

57. Ensure scientific literacy within the curriculum.

As guided and reflected by UNESCO, this is the right time for deep reflection on curriculum, particularly as we struggle against the denial of scientific knowledge and actively fight misinformation. Teachers can help and guide students using various topics via scientific literacy.

58. Webinars

A webinar is an interface over the Internet. A much talked about and explored during the CORONA times globally. The webinar allows interaction between the students and the professors online. When used in a classroom as a medium of teaching, it helps remove the scepticism from the minds of the shy students to raise their hands and ask questions in a classroom full of students—a very effective tool in particular.

59. Process Approach Method

The process approach is a method of thinking applied to understand and plan the sequence and interactions of processes in the system. Teaching here is integrated through a process and the interactions of these processes as part of the teaching and learning system in a classroom scenario.

60. Hands-on hands-On

Hands-on learning is a teaching pattern of imparting education in which children learn by doing themselves. Instead of simply listening to a teacher on the specified subject, the student engages with the subject matter to solve a problem or create something via hands-on experience via engagement and teamwork.

61. Seminars

A seminar is an opportunity to learn or explore learning via interactions. Particularly in academics, a meeting may have several purposes, such as a lecture, where the participants engage in the discussion of an academic subject to gain a better insight into the subject matter. For a typical classroom scenario, it works as an option for learning with pleasure.

62. Chalk and Talk

A Chalk Talk is a much preferred and silent activity that allows all students to reflect on what they know and then share their thinking and wonderings while connecting to their classmates' thoughts. "Chalk & Talk" is a formal teaching method with a blackboard and the teacher's voice as its focal point. This method is used in classrooms across the world. Despite the name, there is no chalk involved with the advent of technology, only paper and pencils, markers or digital devices. Laboratory

The School labs are an excellent place for students, which help them enhance their learning by understanding the theoretical concepts of science taught in classrooms. The set-up of the student-friendly has to be encapsulated. Well-designed laboratories make science experiments fun and help students achieve good academic results. It salutes the framework of learning through demonstrations and hands-on learning.

64. Content Analysis

Content analysis is a research method that allows the qualitative data collected in research to be analysed systematically and reliably so that generalisations can be made about the categories of interest to the researcher. It is one of the ACTIVE RESEARCH activities by educators, and the research findings help deliver learning as a priority for schools.

65. Reciprocal Teaching

Reciprocal teaching is an instructional activity where students become the teacher in small group reading sessions. Common teaching refers to a classroom activity where students are shown strategies to understand a reading better. As one of the periodic models of education, RT helps students learn to guide group discussions using four techniques: summarizing, question generating, clarifying, and predicting in particular.

66. Assignment Method

With the help of the Assignment Method, evaluation based learning is possible. Using this process of assignment method, the teacher delivers an assignment with clear instructions, milestones, objectives and grading criteria based on an outcome that students need to achieve as an activity scheduled over a phase of time. The teacher accordingly monitors and further delivers the feedback to students as they solve the assignment and share the input towards improvement.

67. Micro Teaching

It is a part of teacher training, but it helps students learn a lot. Microteaching can also define as a teaching technique mainly used in teachers‘ pre-service education to train them systematically by allowing them to experiment with main teabehavioursviors real-life life scenarios. It more o less helps as a revision module on the go, which enables teacher trainees to practice a skill by teaching a short lesson to a small number of pupils. Usually,y a micro class of 5 to 10 minutes is taught to four or five fellow students.

68. Mastery Learning

Mastery learning, also known as competency-based teaching, is a set of group-based, individualised teaching and learning strategies based on the preface that students will achieve a high level of understanding in a given domain if given enough time. It ensures that the students obtain mastery of a given topic before moving on to the next unit. The objective is to gain high achievement levels through active instruction, time, and perseverance.

69. Direct Instructions

Direct instruction is a teacher-directed teaching method. This means that the teacher stands in front of a classroom and presents the information. The teachers give explicit, guided instructions to the students. To make it practical and straightforward, direct instruction refers to instructional approaches that are structured, sequenced, and led by teachers, and the presentation of academic content to students by teachers, such as in a lecture or demonstration within the classrooms over a specified interval.

70. Personalised Instruction

It is one of the basic earning and teaching. It refers to instruction-based learning in which the pace of knowledge and the instructional approach are optimised for the needs of each learner. As a Learner Centric and Specific learning format, it fascinates learning towards priority. Learning objectives, instructional strategies, and content (and sequencing) may vary based on learner needs.

71. Recitation

In a general sense, a recitation is an act of reciting from memory or a formal reading of prose or other writing before an audience. The definition of a recitation is the telling of details, or the act of saying something that's bememorisedzed out loud, or the thing that is read.

72. Memorization

It defines the means of learning by self. Many students feel like they simply do not have strong memory skills. Fortunately, though, memorizingmemorisingst for an elite group of people born with the right skills—anyone can train and develop their memorising.

73. Reasoning

This concerns the critical way of learning and exploring the new unknown. Logical reasoning determines if algorithms will work by predicting what happens when the algorithm's steps - and the rules they consist of - are followed. Predictions from each algorithm can be used to compare solutions and decide on the best one.

74. Social-Emotional Learning

Social-emotional learning (SEL) develops self-awareness, self-control, and interpersonal skills important for school, work, and life success. People with strong social-emotional skills prove to be better in Italy's life challenges and benefit academically, professionally, and socially.

75. Instructional scaffolding

Instructional scaffolding is a process through which a teacher supports students to enhance learning and assist in the mastery of tasks. Here, the instructor systematically builds on students' experiences and knowledge while learning the new skills.

CHAPTER THREE

TEACHING AS A PRIORITY

Not all classrooms of today are equipped with the parenting of new-age learning stream, which we observe from taste to tongue the new generation of age. A Teacher, who is now a FACILITATOR in this generation, encapsulates a new order of delivery with the extension of a knowledge society and not a content delivery or an interpretation of book knowledge in real life. The innovation is the ultimate to generate interest in learning for the kids today. It mounts a lot of energy and thoughts to be an innovative educator who is of particular requisite to deliver the knowledge to today's cyber society. The mantra is Engage Me or Enrage Me, from the side of the students at large.

Indeed, the teachers are no longer the sole imparters of knowledge. Still, they need to empower the students to learn at a pace and their leisure through personal learning networks keeping their unique traits of talents and interests. The teachers don't end after the class is over but on the jolt for 24 hours around the cyber linkage or other social networks. There is no wall now or the boundary of learning. The innovative educator has to evolve a personal

learning network for improvement first. It has to reach the students where there is no boundary or limitation in a big way. It is a way to build one's own classroom and network of learning. The change or the shift here is that we can connect and share ideas which are not so in the one to many modes of classroom learning.

The new age imaginative teacher has to be fertile in laminating the knowledge from roots and sharing the same with his students of all ages and figures. It also reflects a Quality Teacher to share the unknown and the unnoticed with the religious sentiments of repute.

The fact lies in the Teacher being an Innovator of traits and essence to explore the attention in the classroom. The priority of taking Education and technology to go together laminates with the questions in our minds, viz. Should we do more or less? What about virtual schools? Interactive whiteboards? Cell phones? Facebook and Twitter? Should we let kids be out there on the 'net? Should we post their pictures? These are legitimate conversations, and each person has to make these kinds of decisions based on their comfort levels and according to the individual child's needs. They must be given an opportunity only when required but as a habit to my knowledge and interest.

The innovative learning is not limited to a physical space but an open learning scenario with a preface to one's comfort in his reading home at home or a TV room at large. It is very much unlike the classroom learning with the same group all day, all the time. Here the community is different, and the learning is more spectacular further. Here the teacher concerned is the one who has to be engaged and involved in the conversations as a leader or a facilitator further.

A priority for the Educators, policymakers and the private sector is the need to strive together and make India a global superpower by 2020. The five year plans in India root to new phases at times, but the delivery is hard to explode in particular.

As per the demands and research, the challenge is to create an integrated education system that:

§ Provides access to quality education that is practical, relevant, customised and effective

§ Can adopt innovative ways (tech-based) to provide faster expansion of opportunities for education to all

§ Looks for bridging the gap between education and employability

§ Promotes social equality/economic viability

One policy is not going to help all. The need of the hour is to have specific guidelines for various levels and areas of education specific to multiple regions.

Requisites of an Innovative Educator

This indicates that you will certainly need to alter your training design. It implies that you will not be pleased with simply resolving a lecture. It could lead to the completion of the lecture as a training gadget for you. To learn if those youngsters are paying attention and engaging with the product, you will need to transform your strategy into an interactive mentor design. You will undoubtedly need to begin speaking to trainees or with trainees and not AT them. Once you do that, the feedback you will obtain and the top quality of your training will undoubtedly boost so considerably that you will certainly never wish to return.

However, simply claiming words right into the air, whether they are listened to or comprehended, truly isn't a mentor? Could you place it in the context of a cook? If you prepare a fantastic dish that is tasty, equip it with the finest of products and existing it with the best setting, is it still an excellent dish if there is no one at the table to value it and no one consuming the plate? No, you are just a cook when the client eats your food and values every subtlety of the taste and the experience of appreciating what you have done. Whether that drives you insane relies on whether you think about the act of training total when you talk or when the trainee realises and recognises what you are stating. Incredibly frequently, when you see an educator talking, you acknowledge that this educator has no issue with whether the pupils are obtaining it. They rule out their task to see to it the trainees comprehend or connect with the product. They are a distribution automobile as well, as if they articulate the lecture efficiently; they have effectively "instructed".

There is a sensation that all speakers experience when they are dealing with a group that, if you considered it significantly, would undoubtedly reach you. It is a sensation that any instructor attempting to give expertise to an area loaded with trainees will surely experience. As well as, if you think of it entirely, it will undoubtedly reach you also. That sensation occurs when you are speaking along as well as you watch out at those empty faces looking up at you, and also you understand that a couple of, some or perhaps every one of those minds behind those faces is paying no focus to you in any way.

Preparing to come to be an instructor has to do with greater than feeling in one's bones, just how to create a lesson strategy and just how to arrange a course area and make a bulletin board system. Ending up being an educator implies you turn into one of those impressive individuals who can take trainees from unenlightened to notified and from unenlightened to absolutely "showed". When it is your contacting us to end up being that type of instructor to chat at pupils without expertise of whether they understand what you are stating in any way is undesirable. That difference drives instructors insane when they feel pupils are not paying attention. To an instructor who wants the genuine act of training, their work refrains until the pupils understand the product and connect with it, examine it, and ultimately comprehend it and make that understanding their own. A lecture not listened to, not recognised, not "instructed" is not instructing in any way; it's simply chatting.

As an academician, I feel that "Everyone is a genius. But if you judge a fish by its ability to climb a tree, it will live its whole life believing that it is stupid." as do one of the inventors of past years.

Cheers and Happy Learning.....

CHAPTER FOUR

DIGITAL TOOLS FOR TEACHING

The essence of Technology identifies learning, and the digital revolution has paced the march of success with the presence of cloud-based computing and deliberations. The nurturing of understanding is encapsulated using the power of technology with WWW- providing learning at pace out of a click of a button at What Ever, When Ever, and Where Ever, to the surprise of many.

Some of the fascinating tools for teaching related to the usage of MS Office at density, with PowerPoint nourishing the majority of the teachers in totality. Still, perfection has to have the stroke of success with the acceptance from the side of the children in particular. The ppt days are over and dead with the lamination of the AI, and the AR segmentation is stated as Artificial Intelligence and Augmented reality in order. The digital lessons provide a sound base with the incorporation of the tools which sound fine with a little hands-on by the teachers but relate to the individual cloud presence by the teacher and a lot of ORM- Online reputation management figure out to the density of understanding and related energy syndrome of clarity among the students at large.

Some of the fascinating and modern applications which relate to the contribution by the teachers figure out for Teaching the Future with the adoption of technology which heavily goes beyond the social networking so-called FACEBOOK and GOOGLE SEARCH options. The incorporated tools for the teachers replicate the understanding and the learning in mass through the doses of the following:

a. *Social Networking and Collaborations:*

The tools here include:

i.

Wikispaces- Teachers may create their Wikispaces to share the teaching and learning materials and the daily lessons.

ii. *Schoology- Used to allow teachers to manage their lessons and engage students.*

iii. *Pinterest- Used to generate assignments, projects and lesson plans.*

iv. *Edmodo- Used as a social networking site.*

v. *Skype- Used for video calling and webcasting.*

vi. *Quora- Used for discussions.*

vii. *Udemy- Used for course uploads and learning.*

a. *Enhancing the Pedagogical Processes with websites in demand like the following:*

i. *Khan Academy- This allows sharing of videos and lessons on various subjects.*

ii. *FunBrain- This allows games on Maths and Logical Reasoning.*

iii. *Animoto- This allows teachers to create simple video-based presentations for the class.*

iv. *Office 365 for Education: Allows free email, shared documents, storage and documentation.*

v. *Kodu- A tool for teaching programming, problem-solving and collaboration in a creative hands-on environment.*

vi. *Teleport- It is a tool which allows downloading all or a part of a website to your computer enabling browsing directly from your hard disk.*

vii. *Youtube Downloader- This is a fascinating tool which allows downloading any youtube video for further viewing and sharing.*

viii. *Yenka- A tool which provides 3Ds experiments and models for mathematics, science and technology.*

c. *Planning Lessons and Projects, attribute to the following tools,*

i. *Prezi- A tool for developing presentations.*

ii. *Planboard- A tool to enable planning and managing daily lessons.*

iii. *Google Docs- Allow sharing documents with modifications by any user logged in.*

iv.

Youtube- A tool which allows videos to be uploaded or downloaded on various topics and tastes.

v.

TEDx is a stand-alone channel with thousands of real-life videos on innovation and activation.

vi.

Photosynth- This helps students learn through interactive 3D experiences.

vii.

meeting- This is a great way to connect and carry out teaching. It is the most powerful web conferencing solution for education, training, meeting webinars and tech support.

d.

Building a Digital Database is possible via the use of the following tools:

i.

Evernote: It is an app designed for note-taking, organising, task lists and archiving.

ii.

Twitter: It is a great platform and a networking service for posting ideas and thoughts with a limitation of words. Tweets are the posts which people share on Twitter.

iii.

Scribd: This is a platform to access everything and anything as information. Once may post or upload data and share it on other social websites.

iv.

Slideshare: This tool allows uploads of presentations and search information related to presentation format and can also be downloaded.

v.

G Suite (Google Apps for Education) offers many functions, including Gmail, Calendar, Classroom, Contacts, Drive, Docs, Forms, Groups, Sheets, Sites, Slides and Hangouts, of great use by the teachers and the schools in particular.

The recruitment is towards catching them young and innocent to the fertile theory of understanding. Majorly, the teachers need to be aware of the above usage in practical for the implementation and relationship towards execution.

Happy Computing and Cyber based teaching!

CHAPTER FIVE

SAFETY IN SCHOOLS AS A PRIORITY

#1

School buildings need to be under surveillance on a 24×7 basis. Assure your CCTV cameras are in working order with the pace of recording. A dimensional view of the recorded data should be analysed to ensure that the charges/ vice principal/ admin staff/ Principal/ Management are routine. The findings must be analysed and queried towards the students' interest in totality.

SAFETY & SECURITY ANCHOR

#2

Emergency exit plans must be in its place. Every floor must have an ENTRY and an EXIT plan on display. Check on locks and barricaders to settle the students with trained, armed guards on duty. Assure there is a public sign designating an official meeting point in the school. It can be called an assembly point; a meeting point is a fixed (safe) place where students can gather or report during an emergency or a fire drill etc.

SAFETY & SECURITY ANCHOR

#3

Appoint Senior Students as FLOOR in charge of managing an easy traffic flow class wise during recess, before and after assembly, and getting over the school. Each floor must have a TEACHER on duty and must be housed with a small staff room occupied by teachers teaching on the respective floor of the classes. Any teacher having a free period must have an eye on the students moving out for any reason.

SAFETY & SECURITY ANCHOR

#4

Preparing students to remain calm in case of attacks is how schools can ensure student safety. This must be practised periodically through MOCK Drills. Ensure inclusive and equitable quality education and promote lifelong learning opportunities for all. The children should be given mock sessions to deal with situations like these and must not react but contribute to a safe exit without fear and anxiety.

SAFETY & SECURITY ANCHOR

#5

Ragging and bullying must be checked regularly. Class Monitors must be coached to inform the Head of School of any such incident in private. Teachers need to be indisputable partners, the front-line actors whom the students trustingly turn to for advice, guidance, for inspiration as they stand on the threshold of young adulthood. The teachers should act like extended family members to the students.

SAFETY & SECURITY ANCHOR

#6

Teachers need to govern their relationship with the students and their parents. They are monitored to be documented using the INTERACTION Register to promote safety as a PRIORITY. To assure liaison and networking, parents need to submit a familphotographsph with the child in the centre for safety and security reasons. This record contributes to knowing the family and the child better.

SAFETY & SECURITY ANCHOR

#7

Schools should also appoint counsellors/ psychologists to help students address trauma/ rage/depression issues. The objective should be to inch each learner a set of values and a sense of moral responsibility and belonging to the nation. The teacher understands the child better and can mould the child to the best format and requirements. Sound advice without AWE is a must for every student by the TEACHER.

SAFETY & SECURITY ANCHOR

#8

Schools need to ensure that students can take care of themselves and tackle situations like abductions/abuse. Assure the spending of money on training people and equipping them with measures of checking CHILD ABUSE/ POCSO or The Protection of Children from Sexual Offences Act (POCSO Act). School management must ensure at least two workshops on CHILD ABUSE in every session.

SAFETY & SECURITY ANCHOR

#9

Schools need to ensure that the food consumed by children on school premises (at the cafeteria or in a school mess) follows stringent measures and guidelines to maintain hygiene. Food served at schools must undergo regular quality checks to ensure that the food is fit for consumption.

SAFETY & SECURITY ANCHOR

#10

Smartphone technology can be used to a school's advantage to maintain students' safety and security. Check for the research adoption of using BLOCKCHAIN Technology to protect students within the campus. The use of AI and Augmented Reality is also on the cards. Technology adoption is hence a requisite for running a school peacefully.

SAFETY & SECURITY ANCHOR

#11

Install EFFECTIVE CCTV Cameras in all Nooks and Corners of the School Premises, including the entry of the WASHROOMS and entry/ exit points of the school. It is suggested to be installed in every classroom, and the parents should be given access to the feed through a mobile phone app.

SAFETY & SECURITY ANCHOR

#12

The School Compound Should Be Fenced and Gated. Guards should be on ROUND duty with proper LATHIS and TORCH with a whistle. The respective locations of these guards should be monitored using the GPRS tracking system.

SAFETY & SECURITY ANCHOR

#13

There Should Be Security Personal Stationed at the School Gate and must MONITOR the CCTV Camera on the found. The Entry/ Exit REGISTER should be marked and duly signed regularly for ENTRY and EXIT.

SAFETY & SECURITY ANCHOR

#14

Clearance Should Be Given to Any Visitor before Entering the School Premises by the person responsible for the MEETING. Teachers must stand guard in front of classroom doors, regularly watching for misconduct during the Parent/ Teacher Meetings.

SAFETY & SECURITY ANCHOR

#15

Students and Workers Should Always Be In Possession of their ID cards and valid security IDs. Police officers need to be given the authority to conduct random pre-emptive searches of students' lockers and personal property—a check on driving licenses and vehicles also needs to be monitored.

SAFETY & SECURITY ANCHOR

#16

Proper Security Check Must Be Conducted Before Employing Teachers and Other Employees. Schools must conduct periodic criminal history checks of school employees during their employment. In addition, the school must establish policies requiring school employees to report any arrests for crimes to their school employees within 24 hours of such arrests.

SAFETY & SECURITY ANCHOR

#17

Students Should Be Trained On Security Related Subjects/ incidences/ scenario. The school must be a place in practice where students develop both socially and emotionally. Staff members and the students should know WHAT TO DO IN A CRISIS? There has to be a collaboration with the POLICE.

SAFETY & SECURITY ANCHOR

#18

A Leadership Team and a Security Club Should Be Formed in the School with REGULAR safety and security guidelines. The team should include all types of individuals from the school, community and others. These individuals should develop school-wide prevention plans, analyse the needs assessment, and formulate short and long-term goals.

SAFETY & SECURITY ANCHOR

#19

Only the Parents of Students or Someone Duly Assigned Should Be Allowed to Pickup Students from the School. Staff must be trained to recognise the parents, and their training ensures understanding, support and use of a school-wide violence prevention plan. The constanmovementng makes the students and the faculty comfortable with the crisis plan.

SAFETY & SECURITY ANCHOR

#20

Central Security Alarm Should Be Installed in the School Premises. A mock drill for the same must be carried out from time to time. There has to be a complete 360-degree integrated security solution from intrusion detection security systems, video surveillance and fire alarm test and inspections to mass notification, emergency communication, an indication of any Terrorist Attack and everything in between.

SAFETY & SECURITY ANCHOR

#21

Students' Bags Should Be Searched from Time to Time to Prevent Them from Bringing Dangerous Weapons into the School. These random searches must be based on unique, school-wide needs to ensure school safety and should be truly random. A random search can not be done to target any individual child in the school.

SAFETY & SECURITY ANCHOR

#22

StudentsStudents' Activities should be strictly monitored to prevent them from Joining Secret Cults. Individual traits of the children need to be monitored, and constant positive reinforcement and motivation need to be given. This is possible only if the child feels connected to the Teacher. Monitoring activates the possibility for classroom development.

SAFETY & SECURITY ANCHOR

#23

Students Should Be Encouraged To Report any Suspicious Moves or Persons within the School Premises to the School Management. Teachers should connect with other teachers that interact with the child in the next grade and help work on the child's developmental process. We must provide various reporting options like anonymous reporting strategies through websites, text, phones, designated teachers, counsellors, and peers.

SAFETY & SECURITY ANCHOR

#24

Students Should Only Be Allowed To Leave the School Premises Only When They Have a Pass from the Security Post. No child should be allowed to walk home without prior consent from a parent or guardian. Parents must understand that it is their responsibility of theirs' and not the thschoolsol once their children have left the school premises.

SAFETY & SECURITY ANCHOR

#25

People Should Be Discouraged from Loitering or Parking Their Cars outside the School fence. The schools should encourage parents to adopt the carpool system to drop and pick up their children. This may reduce traffic chaos outside schools and ease the flow of vehicles. The priority is to gel with the society/ public/ neighbourhood injunction for ease of business and transit within the security framework.

SAFETY & SECURITY ANCHOR

#26

The use of mobile phones in school settings or environments is a topic of debate. Students Should Not Be Allowed to Make Use of Mobile Phones within the School Premises. There should not be any BLANKET Ban on phones, but when in emergencies, the children should be allowed to use them. They should only have access to a mobile phone where there is a need to contact parents/ guardians in an emergency.

SAFETY & SECURITY ANCHOR

#27

Students and PARENTS Should Be Issued Access Cards with the BIO-METRIC system and recognition. This system can purchase food and drink in the dining hall and use the library to manage the loan and submission of books issued earlier utilising the credit.

SAFETY & SECURITY ANCHOR

#28

Kids Should Be Taught Not to Talk to Strangers within or even outside the school campus. The unfortunate incidents of abductions and molestations in and outside the schools with our students make it more important to educate our kids about Mr Danger Stranger and how and why they should continue to be vigilant all their life.

SAFETY & SECURITY ANCHOR

#29

Teach teachers To Be Vigilant on issues related to CYBER Bullying, CHILD Abuse and Racism. The child Abuse Identification and Reporting workshop is essential. The Child Abuse Identification & Reporting Workshop must be a priority for both the PARENTS and the Faculty.

SAFETY & SECURITY ANCHOR

#30

Teach the school's emergency procedures via YOUTUBE Videos/ Simulation Games/ Mock Drills as a part of the ROUTINE exercise. Children should know how to respond to any EMERGENCY. Online drills sessions must be there during SUPW periods in standard as an exercise in practice.

SAFETY & SECURITY ANCHOR

#31

Teach the Travel Routes to and from the school for nearby locations. POICE and relief/ help/ emergency numbers must be landmarked and earmarked at every nook and corner of the school around the campus, and children and staff should be proactive for any assistance.

SAFETY & SECURITY ANCHOR

#32

All stakeholders need to be well-versed in school security and safety measures. A regular orientation towards any new building and exit and entry plans should be mentioned via exclusive videos and manuals to all the stakeholders to face any emergency.

SAFETY & SECURITY ANCHOR

#33

Overall, the environment is the most significant enabler of learning. It can be created by focuthreesing on three major components- the teachers, the technologies and the curriculum. Teacher tricritical is the critical component of the Finland Model and the creative and customised curriculum. The "one size fits all" Indian education system and rote memory-based exams only produce parrots, not creative thinkers.

SAFETY & SECURITY ANCHOR

#34

Staff must be informed periodically on Student Safety and Behavioural Issues. The teachers should not limit their interaction with a class for a year but track the development of the children as they move on. The whole teaching and learning process should be immersed in a "facilitating" environment that is not very easy to create. Just look at the home environment. It is all about control and command. This is where our children get started. Hence home, school environment and social values have to be in sync to produce the Finland system.

SAFETY & SECURITY ANCHOR

#35

Any Loose Electrical Wires must be tended to immediately. The student council's admin/ staff/ prefect/ member on floor duty must inform the concerned authority of any short circuit or loose wiring on the campus.

SAFETY & SECURITY ANCHOR

#36

Regular structural audits must be conducted of the school building. There has to be a timely inspection of FIRE ALARMS/ FIRE FIGHTING equipment to be in place and in working order to handle any emergency. This must be tested via MOCK Drills on and off.

SAFETY & SECURITY ANCHOR

#37

The Schools must ensure the railings and pathways are sturdy along the staircase and corridors. They must be well lit and guarded by an Adult during dispersal. Wherever practical, separate access points should be provided for people and vehicles to ensure the safe flow to and from the school boundary. From the fencing around its perimeter to the main entrance gates, visitors get a clear impression of a school's commitment to safety and security before entering its grounds.

SAFETY & SECURITY ANCHOR

#38

Toilets at school ensure privacy and safety. Going to a school lacking proper basic facilities, like toilets, could be one of the most frustrating situations for many hence the entrance to the TOILETS needs to be monitored. Every student's move around the un-manned/ restricted places must be observed and checked using the CCTV Camera.

SAFETY & SECURITY ANCHOR

#39

School ID cards are intended to identify elementary, high school, or college students to prove their membership in the school or college. Badges and name tags must be mandatory for the TEACHING and NON-TEACHING STAFF. Assure meeting up of the SOCIAL and EMOTIONAL needs of the children through PEP talk and interactions and may include HOME VISITS by the teachers.

SAFETY & SECURITY ANCHOR

#40

Police Verification of the Teaching and Non-Teaching Staff should always be undertaken. This may include checking the stakeholders' cultural and Parental Background of the stakeholders too as documented information. Ensuring employment of support staff only from authorised agencies and maintaining proper records is another one of the guidelines.

SAFETY & SECURITY ANCHOR

#41

CBSE Quote

"Schools must get the psychometric evaluation done for all the staff. Such verification and evaluation for non-teaching teams -such as bus drivers, conductors, peons and other support staff -may be done very carefully and in a detailed manner,"

Psychometric Evaluation of the Teaching and Non-Teaching Staff should always be undertaken.

SAFETY & SECURITY ANCHOR

#42

The playground should be aesthetically designed and maintained regularly with opportunities for multi courts and games with physical activities. Assure every child's attendance to be marked thrice a day and messages sent to parents if their children are absent. Assure No child should be punished in such a way that could cause mental or physical trauma.

SAFETY & SECURITY ANCHOR

#43

The classrooms must be aesthetically designed with equipped ICT facilities and support mechanisms. Regularly update licenses for the software in use with proper anti-virus and a check on CYBER bullying with FIREWALLS installed in systems.

SAFETY & SECURITY ANCHOR

#44

A check on having enough TOILETS separately for girls and boys/ Male and Female Staff, safe drinking water, medical room and counselling room. Among the preventive measures suggested for girls' safety are separate washrooms for boys and girls at a suitable distance and the deployment of a female attendant in the girls' bathroom.

SAFETY & SECURITY ANCHOR

#45

All the students must be given Psychiatric Support and Counselling, particularly on Cyber Bullying.

School counsellors should teach sex education classes, provide information to students about bullying and offer seminars on study skills.

They MUST collaborate with the teachers, parents and special educators to create a healthy learning environment that makes them feel comfortable.

SAFETY & SECURITY ANCHOR

#46

Busses should follow clear mandates, including the seat to student ratio, display of emergency numbers, and tracking system. A female teacher or attendant should accompany a girl if she must leave the school for an exam or another event, and the school bus female attendant should not leave the bus unless the last girls are dropped to their destination.

SAFETY & SECURITY ANCHOR

#47

Aesthetically designed furniture should be age-appropriate in classrooms at different levels. The school building should be prepared for natural light and ventilation inflow.

SAFETY & SECURITY ANCHOR

#48

A school safety committee should be constituted to ensure and monitor safety practices. Student Council should be directed to shoulder the additional responsibility for the safety and security of the students. The school must also have a vigilance committee comprising parents, and the schools should follow it.

SAFETY & SECURITY ANCHOR

#49

Visit the Police Station by the school's kids to understand the role of police in our daily lives and their contribution to the safety and security of the country's citizens. Schools need to take cognisance of safety issues as per the guidelines set by the boards and the government.

SAFETY & SECURITY ANCHOR

#50

There has to be a regular METAL DETECTOR CHECK for Visitors. Assure school stakeholders are frequently trained to manage emergencies and disasters with good practice in conducting mock drills and evacuation drills.

SAFETY & SECURITY ANCHOR

#51

There has to be a documented Safety Norm for every LABORATORY in the school. Check for the availability of facilities supporting differently-abled students. Students should never work in a science lab without their teachers. Students must be made to wear safety goggles, lab coats, and shoes in the science laboratory. In school science labs, loose clothes, sandals, and loose hair should be a strict NO.

SAFETY & SECURITY ANCHOR

#52

Every student in the school and the teacher/ employee must know how to operate a fire fighting Equipment installed on the campus. Identify the TWO closest exits and all possible evacuation routes. Know locations of fire alarms and how to use them. Teachers and Students must report vandalised fire equipment to campus security.

SAFETY & SECURITY ANCHOR

#53

Regular Inspections of Fire Fighting Equipment must be on the cards. Assure stringent provisions for emergency management are in place for all types of FIRE and alarm during an emergency and call for nearest POLICE STATIONS and mention significant PHONE NUMBERS in place.

SAFETY & SECURITY ANCHOR

#54

The Annual Curriculum plan of the school should integrate the academic, social, physical and emotional needs of the children.

Identify what hazards are likely to affect the area in and around your school. Determine the severity of the impact of each identified hazard. Students and staff must be trained on using the plan and their responsibilities in a given response.

SAFETY & SECURITY ANCHOR

#55

The infrastructure, including Computer Labs, Science Labs, and Math Labs, must be appropriate and meet expected standards ALL THE TIME. Areas where students congregate while waiting for buses and associated pedestrian paths, are adequate to avoid overcrowding. Access into each building is controllable through designated entry points. If possible, identify one entry point for visitors.

SAFETY & SECURITY ANCHOR

#56

The school must have adequate medical facilities and be equipped with a nurse/ doctor to handle medical and other emergencies. Create at least one Administrator Emergency Tool Kit for each school building. Develop and distribute emergency response guides for each classroom. Establish and document procedures for providing students and staff access to mental health services.

SAFETY & SECURITY ANCHOR

#57

Restrooms, toilets, laboratory, playground, and classrooms must be CLEAN, AIRY, and WELL. Schools must also have ramps and need to admit students of disadvantaged groups and have SPECIAL Educators to assist the needy concerned. Send at least two girls/ boys to the washroom at a time so that in case of an emergency, one of them can raise the alarm.

SAFETY & SECURITY ANCHOR

#58

There should be separate TOILETS for Female and Male Staff. The school must also ensure adequate medical facilities and be equipped to handle medical and other emergencies. Without proper cleaning, washrooms can become breeding grounds for germs that can spread disease throughout the school population.

SAFETY & SECURITY ANCHOR

#59

The Library should be airy and be equipped with an EMERGENCY Alarm System and Fire Fighting Equipment.

Use posters and bulletin boards to emphasise potential dangers and safety procedures.

Post legible, accurate emergency numbers and procedures.

SAFETY & SECURITY ANCHOR

#60

The school must take the initiative to Conservation of Environment and take MAJOR initiatives in IMPLEMENTING Waste Management Practices. Use organic waste for composting and teach students about how it works. Schools can use the compost in the school gardens, saving on the cost of fertiliser and other chemicals. Schools could set up worm farms, which can be used to teach parts of the curriculum.

SAFETY & SECURITY ANCHOR

#61

The school should have a provision for

DIFFERENTLY ABLED INDIVIDUALS should provide a conducive working environment with growth opportunities. Students in wheelchairs attend public schools more and more regularly.

Schools must adhere to the norms for assistance to these children.

SAFETY & SECURITY ANCHOR

#62

There has to be a sense of SAFETY and SECURITY in the School, with regular evacuation drills being carried out from time to time.

Ref: Quote: Example

Fire Drill PM, #5 of 5, the School Year 2016-2017 3.21.17 @ 1:40 PM Evacuation/ Shelter Time: 1min, 00sec Participants: 45 total participants Drill Conducted by: Loretta Tobolske-Horn, Greenfield Principal Acknowledgement of Completed Drill: On File at HCISD Office, 310 W. Bacon Street, Hillsdale

SAFETY & SECURITY ANCHOR

#63

Schools Need an eye beyond CCTV Cameras.

A must check by teachers and knowing each child by the first name is very important. In addition, there has to be a HEALTH CARD for every child with all MEDICAL records in the count.

SAFETY & SECURITY ANCHOR

#64

Schools must ensure all records in the school diary should be updated and recorded for easy reference. Parents must be communicated about their child's health issues, what so ever of PRIORITY.

"Nevertheless, no school can work well for children if parents and teachers do not act in

partnership on behalf of the children's best interests. Parents have every right to understand what is happening to their children at school, and teachers are responsible for sharing that……": - Dorothy Cohen.

SAFETY & SECURITY ANCHOR

#65

The schools should advocate, model, and teach safe, legal, and ethical use of digital information and technology; promote and model responsible social interaction related to technology and knowledge; celebrate Cyber Security Week and conduct activities to create awareness through cyber clubs.

SAFETY & SECURITY ANCHOR

#66

Check the Cyber Bullying, If any, through ONE on ONE interactions and observatory efforts. Frequent CYBER ethics sessions need to be observed and organised for the students, parents and other stakeholders. There has to be a digital technology program in places like ERP which should serve as an interactive medium 'between the educators and the guardians."

SAFETY & SECURITY ANCHOR

#67

Check on CHILD ABUSE in practice by using friendly options with the students by asking them to share the uncomfortable moments they feel being around the school. It is up to us to ensure our children grow up in environments that build confidence, friendship, security, and happiness, irrespective of their family circumstances or backgrounds. Keeping children safe from harm requires a vigilant and informed community.

SAFETY & SECURITY ANCHOR

#68

Check on SECURITY agency people with their I-Cards, Lathis, Umbrella, Torch and Safety Belts. There has to be a fitness MEDICAL certificate available for all guards on duty.

SAFETY & SECURITY ANCHOR

#69

Any water is logging in the washroom or around the washroom/ corridors. A check is required on priority. Well-designed school restrooms can enhance student health, deter misbehaviour, and conserve resources. The initiative should be that the children bring these behaviours home, thereby acting as agents of change in their communities.

SAFETY & SECURITY ANCHOR

#70

Floors surfaces chipped or carpets in Music Rooms worn out with spots or holes may lead to sudden slipping of the children and this balancing. Safety precautions peculiar to any new lesson should be emphasised at the start of the class.

SAFETY & SECURITY ANCHOR

#71

Observe if the Aisles are free of boxes, wastebaskets, chairs and other obstacles that may impede traffic within the campus. Check on the internal flooring of the classroom, lighting in the school and the children are aware of the evacuation drill, and the classroom is naturally ventilated. Ideally, the classrooms must have rules towards letting the students set their climate of respect and responsibility.

SAFETY & SECURITY ANCHOR

#72

Check on whether the doors have stoppers in classrooms. Students must check on their behaviours, and Teachers must help students correct their behaviours and help them understand violating the rules results in consequences. They should be told to respect ground rules, and the kids should feel free to discuss issues without fear.

SAFETY & SECURITY ANCHOR

#73

Check on POWER sockets in classrooms, if any, that must be out of the reach of the children. Assure proper Earth wire towards protection against electric shock. The children should be told to stand clear of any fallen power lines. Remove unused wall outlets and apply tape over new plug holes or cord holders. Also, ensure they get dry when they come out of the swimming pools in the classrooms to operate computers or any electrical device in particular.

SAFETY & SECURITY ANCHOR

#74

Five S in action with a special marking for FAN (F) and TUBE (T) as special mentions on switchboards within classrooms. A check update is required. 5S is a workplace organisation method that uses a list of five Japanese words: seiri, seitan, season, seiketsu, and shitsuke. These have been translated as "Sort", "Set In Order", "Shine", "Standardize", and "Sustai.n."

SAFETY & SECURITY ANCHOR

#75

Evaluate the students' MEDICAL history from time to time, and teachers must study the child's health record as part of the routine. They must have a form of food allergy, physical disability or if there is a cause or a case of bullying, with a keep of the information conveyed to the Head of the school and the Principal in the loop.

SAFETY & SECURITY ANCHOR

#76

Are Staircases well lit?

"You can't study or learn if you don't feel safe at school."

—Bill Jenkins, director of Student Services, Millard Public Schools (Omaha, Neb.)

The school MUST have an EMERGENCY plan A and B and MUST not be making decisions under DURESS that they have not practised.

"Students not only understand 'see something, say something,' but they also know who to tell and feel comfortable approaching them."

—Rex Barrett, acting director of security services, Prince George's County (Md.) Public Schools

SAFETY & SECURITY ANCHOR

#77

Are Staircases free from litter, spills or clutter? Assure children travel on the right side of staircases and hallways. Appealing staircases will encourage use. The teachers and the charges must monitor slops and falls, sharp edges and the assurance of up to date maintenance.

SAFETY & SECURITY ANCHOR

#78

Do Teachers or Students stand on some stand or ladders in any case for teaching/ demonstrating, which needs supervision and support?. If need be, the assistance from students can be supported but under sucontrolThis is practical, real-life learning and experience for them.

SAFETY & SECURITY ANCHOR

#79

Do Students/ Teachers RUN in the area after assembly or during the getting over of the school? A must check, and the solution is drawn for an easy and organised exit and entry to the assembly ground. The students should be guided during the dispersal. There has to be a public-address system to ensure timely and safe evacuation during an emergency.

SAFETY & SECURITY ANCHOR

#80

Children should be briefed about safe touch and unsafe touch, avoiding interaction with strangers and reporting any and every concern, however irrelevant it may seem. Also, any behaviour change has to be communicated to the parents. There has to be an open communication channel with the students, and they should be given a patient hearing for even the smallest of matters.

SAFETY & SECURITY ANCHOR

#81

The buses and other school transport should be IDENTITY marked with helpline phone numbers, and students should be issued a Bus Badge with Bus Route Number. They should use only the allotted bus and bus stop. Boarding and alighting from the bus should be done in silence and orderly.

SAFETY & SECURITY ANCHOR

#82

Computers and SERVERS need supervision in LABS/ deserted rooms. Passwords and WIFI should be protected and activated timely for execution. Original Software should be preferred to assure attack of Malware or Virus in particular. Students should not be allowed to use external drives.

SAFETY & SECURITY ANCHOR

#83

No Strangers should be allowed to Meet Children. No stranger, driver or family friend should be allowed to pick the children up. The Principals' helpline should be used to inform any irregularity. Students should not be allowed to drive motorised vehicles such as cars, scooters and motorcycles within or outside the school.

SAFETY & SECURITY ANCHOR

#84

Do all employees know the exit locations and directions when in an EMERGENCY? EAP or Emergency Assembly Points should be located away from the building. Fire Exit Symbols should be in place for immediate evacuation using the nearest escape route. The schools must ENSURE School Building Level Emergency Preparedness and Response Plan.

SAFETY & SECURITY ANCHOR

#85

Are fire drills conducted regularly? Check on Training of Task Forces, Demonstration, Mock Drills, develop emergency resource contact inventory for human resource, transport and tools required dealing with emergency response, Hazard Hunt Programmes, Training for First Aid Search and Rescue, and building evacuation drills regularly. It is recommended to prepare a detailed floor evacuation plan and conduct a mock exercise for an earthquake or a fire to test emergency plans and update the findings.

SAFETY & SECURITY ANCHOR

#86

Assure a QUICK background check of visitors in the schools and information explored via IDs'. Involve PARENTS as partners in Safety and Security Mechanism in action. Assure Disaster Management in Education and formal training/workshops for all the stakeholders to mainstream the discipline of disaster risk management.

SAFETY & SECURITY ANCHOR

#87

Are all incidents/ accidents adequately reported, investigated and documented? Check on provision to parents the information on school's emergency policies and procedures to further update on Emergency Notification Cards in the almanacks. The plans must execute as an EMERGENCY plan and keep the students safe when crisis strikes.

SAFETY & SECURITY ANCHOR

#88

Is medical help readily available? Assure procedure to evacuate the building, evacuate the premises, shift to temporary shelter, safeguard students and staff, notify parents, notify media, provide transportation and debrief procedures timely and appropriately. Make the vital PHONE numbers available in case of emergency to be painted on display around the campus.

SAFETY & SECURITY ANCHOR

#89

Enhancements. Employees need to be empowered to check and identify any uncommon person in safety. The school must appoint a PRO or a public information officer to provide information and the current status of the situation to the parents and other inquiring parties in case of an emergency.

SAFETY & SECURITY ANCHOR

#90

VISITORS Batch to be given to all who wish to come to the school during office hours. Also, ensure the emergency plans need to be reviewed and revised regularly. Make it a living document with modifications in a requisite timely. The paper should address prevention/ mitigation, preparedness, response and recovery aspects.

SAFETY & SECURITY ANCHOR

#91

Assure of conducting a preliminary assessment of preparedness measures of each school building. There has to be a review of the building layout and the surrounding areas for the safe evacuation of the students. Also, inspect equipment to ensure it operates during crises. Develop a command structure for responding to an emergency.

SAFETY & SECURITY ANCHOR

#92

Assure children walk on the side of the corridors to ensure everyone gets to classes safely. Make sure the good plans are never finished. They need to be constantly updated based on the experience, changing vulnerabilities, and assessing current capabilities. One must carry out shelter assessment needs for various situational responses. An emergency supply inventory should be checked and updated as per the expiry.

SAFETY & SECURITY ANCHOR

#93

Assure children and any adult, RESPECT, if someone has an injury, excuse not to get in their way of walking. One must be aware and prepared; not being SCARED should be the priority. Every room in the school should have a map posted identifying two ways out. The exit paths should be obvious and kept free of obstruction.

SAFETY & SECURITY ANCHOR

#94

Follow the rules to go up and down the stairs. Once everyone has safely exited the building during an emergency, they should remain outside at a predetermined location until the 'all clear' green signal has been given to enter the installation again.

SAFETY & SECURITY ANCHOR

#95

Include TERRORISM THREAT in School Syllabi.

All schools up to the secondary level should include this as a very critical issue in their syllabi. It should be as compulsory for students as military service, which is mandatory for the youths in Israel. This is a security step towards safety and security scenarios within schools.

SAFETY & SECURITY ANCHOR

#96

Assure and Make Sure there is a SILENCE ZONE in the school to monitor and assure discipline. Let the staff and students follow the same religion. Quiet Zones in schools and classrooms are an easy way to help meet a need that all students have at one time or another. The need to be able to take a break from the noise and pressure of social interaction and recharge.

SAFETY & SECURITY ANCHOR

#97

Let the children play SMART and follow the elementary playground safely. Let the children follow for their turns in line. Assure attention by the teachers on swings, slides and other equipment. They must actively supervise students on playgrounds. Assure of age-appropriate playground equipment. The children should only be allowed in proper attire and choose a garden with shock-absorbing surfaces.

SAFETY & SECURITY ANCHOR

#98

Do you have a designated drop off and pick up area at your school? A defined pick up and drop points for walkers, bus takers and Parents' fetch & drop. The guided line-wise provision has to be a routine for average dispersal on all days and special requirements for the rainy/ emergency days accordingly. Specified Drop-off spots are locations near primary schools where parents can drop off or pick up their children.

SAFETY & SECURITY ANCHOR

#99

Are safety rules displayed and visible?

Check the updates on Step up for Students' Health, promoting a healthy school ecosystem. The schools need to provide a monthly calendar for educating each child on hygiene, nutrition, stress and vision through educational videos and hands-on activities integrated via guest lectures and workshops.

About The Authors

Dheeraj Mehrotra, MS, MPhil, PhD (Education Management) honoris causa., a white and a

yellow belt in SIX SIGMA, a Certified NLP Business Diploma holder, is an Educational Innovator, Author, with expertise in Six Sigma In Education, Academic Audits, Neuro-Linguistic Programming (NLP), Total Quality Management In Education, an Experiential Educator, a CBSE Resource towards School Assessment (SQAA), CCE, JIT, Five S, and KAIZEN. He has authored over 40 books on Computer Science for ICSE/ ISC/ CBSE Students, over 60 books of academic interest for the field of education excellence, and Six Sigma. A former Principal at De Indian Public School, New Delhi, (INDIA) with an ample teaching experience of over Two Decades, he is a certified Trainer for Quality Circles/ TQM in Education and QCI Standards for School Accreditation/ Six Sigma in Education. He has also been honoured with the President of India's National Teacher Award in the year 2006 and the Best Science Teacher State Award (By the Ministry of Science and Technology, State of UP), Innovation in Education for his inception of Six Sigma In Education by Education Watch, New Delhi and Education World- Best Teacher Award, BOLT Learner Teacher Award by Air India, 'Innovation in Education Award 2016' by Higher Education Forum (HEF), Gujarat Chapter, among others. He can be visited at www.authordheerajmehrotra.com

Janaka Kamalgoda is an educationist from Sri Lanka. He is the Managing Director and the Chief Executive Officer at the South Asian International Institute of Higher Education, at Colombo. Also a Senior Psychological Counselor and a member of the board of Management, National Apprentice and Industrial Training Authority and President, South Asian International Association for Early Childhood Care and Development (SAIA4ECCD).

Books By The Same Author

Enter Caption

9 798887 170930

Printed by Libri Plureos GmbH in Hamburg,
Germany